Children Do,
Grownups Don't

NORMA SIMON
pictures by Helen Cogancherry

Albert Whitman & Company
Niles, Illinois

Also by Norma Simon
All Kinds of Families
Cats Do, Dogs Don't
Cuando me enojo . . . (I Was So Mad, *Spanish edition*)
Elly the Elephant
Go Away, Warts!
How Do I Feel?
I Know What I Like
I'm Busy, Too
I Was So Mad
I Wish I Had My Father
Nobody's Perfect, Not Even My Mother
Oh, That Cat!
The Saddest Time
We Remember Philip
What Do I Do? (*English/Spanish*)
What Do I Say?
Where Does My Cat Sleep?
Why Am I Different?

Library of Congress Cataloging-in-Publication Data

Simon, Norma.
      Children do, grownups don't.

      Summary: Contrasts the behavior and activities of
children and grownups in such areas as eating,
selection of television programs, and sleeping.
      1. Children—Juvenile literature.   2. Adulthood—
Juvenile literature.   3. Human behavior—Juvenile
literature.   [1. Children and adults.   2. Behavior]
I. Cogancherry, Helen, ill.   II. Title.
HQ781.S52   1987   305.2'3   87-2205
ISBN 0-8075-1144-7 (lib. bdg.)

Text ©1987 by Norma Simon
Illustrations ©1987 by Helen Cogancherry
Published in 1987 by Albert Whitman & Company
Published simultaneously in Canada by General Publishing, Limited, Toronto

For Ed and my Wellfleet elementary school friends,
with loving appreciation for sharing your ideas **N.S.**
To Lauren **H.C.**

Kids like to play outdoors,
even on drizzly days.
They don't care if they get dirty and wet.

Grownups would rather stay inside
and be clean and warm and dry.

Grownups like to eat strange things—
liver and cabbage and smelly cheese.

Children think peanut butter sandwiches are best,
and they don't like liver or cabbage or smelly cheese much.

Kids chew hunks of bubble gum.
They blow *humungus* sticky bubbles.

Grownups only do this when other grownups aren't watching!

Kids play with toys in bubble baths.
Grownups don't—
did you ever see a grownup with a rubber duck?

Some grownups get bald,
like my grandpa.
Children have lots of hair
(except bald babies).

Children lose their teeth and grow bigger new ones.
Grownups don't grow new teeth.
If they lose them,
they have to get false teeth from the dentist.

Grownups can reach high places
and carry heavy loads.
Kids can't, but they can fit into tight spaces
where grownups would get stuck.

Grownups need grownup clothes.
Kids wear kid-sized clothes.

Children give out lots of valentines
and get lots of them back.
Grownups get just a few.

Grownups like getting shirts and socks for presents.
Not kids—they like *toys*.

Grownups like to watch the news on TV.
They read newspapers and books with lots of words.
Children love to watch cartoons,
and they like books with pictures in them.

Grownups get lots of mail.
They call some "junk"
and throw it away.

Kids love to open anything with their name on it—
especially postcards, birthday cards,
party invitations,
and letters from Grandma and Grandpa.

Children make houses from boxes
refrigerators and stoves come in.
Grownups think a box is just a box.

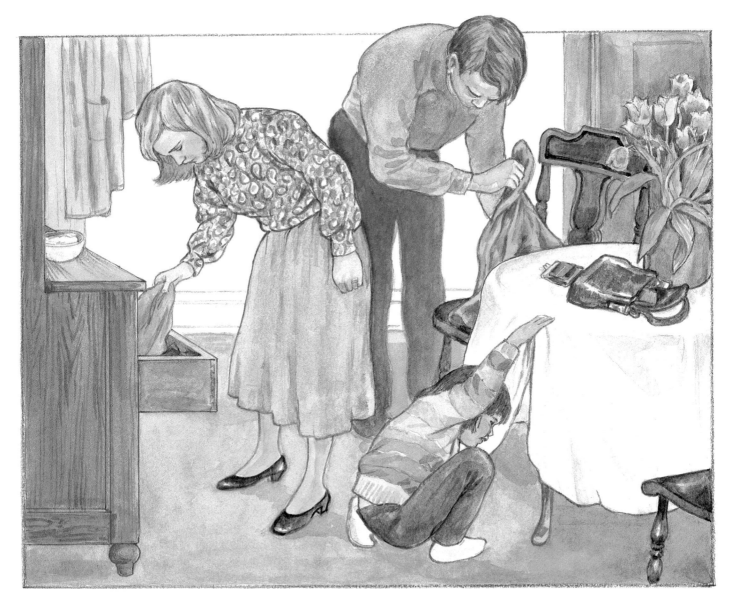

Kids get grumpy when they can't find their sneakers
and it's time to go out.
How do grownups act when they lose their car keys?

Kids like to sleep in all sorts of places.

Grownups like to sleep in bed.

Grownups take care of children when they're feeling sick.
They put Band-Aids on and call the doctor
and give you medicine.
They hug you and make you feel better.

Children just play they are doctors and nurses.

(But when my mom had the flu, I made her tea and toast.
She said it helped a lot.)

Grownups pay taxes and bills and complain about them.
Children don't.

They worry about being late for the school bus,
taking report cards home,
and overdue library books they can't find anywhere.

Children play in the snow.
They make angels and snowmen and forts.

Grownups have to shovel snow.
Sometimes they grumble and call it hard work.

Children sleep with cozy stuffed animals.
Grownups don't,

but I bet they wish they could.

(Once I lent Mom my littlest teddy bear.
She said it made her feel better.)

Children go to preschool and kindergarten
and grades one, two, three, four, five, six, seven, eight.
Grownups are finished with all those grades,
unless they are teachers.

They help with homework and tell stories
about when they went to school, in the olden days.

Children grow and keep on growing.
Grownups are all grown up.
And if they're very lucky,
they have children of their own
to take care of and love.